The Shape of Our Faces No Longer Matters

Poems by Gerardo Mena

Southeast Missouri State University Press • 2014
Military-Service Literature Series

The Shape of Our Faces No Longer Matters by Gerardo Mena

Softcover: $14.00
ISBN: 978-0-9883103-6-0

First published in 2014 by
Southeast Missouri State University Press
One University Plaza, MS 2650
Cape Girardeau, MO 63701
www6.semo.edu/universitypress

Cover photography by Bryan Ernst
Cover Design: Liz Lester

Southeast Missouri State University Press's Military-Service
Literature Series is sponsored in partnership with the Missouri
Humanities Council and with support from the National Endow-
ment for the Humanities.

The Shape of Our Faces No Longer Matters

Acknowledgements

Grateful acknowledgement is made to the following publications in which these poems have originally appeared or are forthcoming.

Barely South Review, Baltimore Review, Best New Poets 2011, Cider Press Review, Cream City Review, Diagram, Four Way Review, Hawai'i Review, Iron Horse Review, Louisiana Review, The Medulla Review, New Mexico Poetry Review, Ninth Letter, Permafrost, Poetry East, Poets & Writers Magazine, Prairie Schooner's Online Digital Project, *Proud to Be: Writing by American Warriors, Raleigh Review, Steamticket, Spillway Magazine,* and *War, Literature and the Arts.*

"So I Was a Coffin" won first prize in the "2010 War Poetry" contest sponsored by *Winningwriters.*

"Baring the Trees" won first prize in the "National Veterans Writing Contest" sponsored by Missouri Humanities Council, Warriors Arts Alliance, and Southeast Missouri State University Press.

"War Haiku (B-Side)" won first prize in the "2011 Penumbra Haiku Contest" sponsored by *Seven Hills Review.*

Contents

III. Welcome Home, or the Sound of Your Blood Humming

Dedication

An infinite ocean of gratitude is extended to the following people that have made this book a reality:

To my parents for a lifetime of support in every single wild hair-brained idea that I've ever had (like joining Spec Ops or wanting to write poetry).

To Brian Turner for those simple words that ignited a fire within me.

To the amazing men of 3rd Reconnaissance Battalion, specifically Trey Maxwell for being a great friend and the best damn medical vehicle driver to ever walk this earth, Maxwell Scott for all the great laughs, John Murray for showing me what determination and balls of steel actually looks like, T.J. Edwards for being the toughest guy I've ever met, Kip Morey for always having my back through everything, Cameron Crews for letting me name my first-born son after his awesomeness, and Sean and Sarah Lennon for listening to my whining, getting me drunk often, and letting me use their boards to surf.

To the incredibly talented and kind mentors that I've had along the way, specifically Aliki Barnstone and her amazing Greek family dinners during workshop, Jessica Garratt for understanding that sometimes you have to write really bad poems before the good ones surface, and John Nieves . . . well, there's not enough room in this book without writing another book about all the help, patience, and motivation that John has shown me. This book would not be here without him.

And finally to my kids: Avery and Cameron. Daddy did it!

We are dirty and proud and lonely—
we sad and hardened few.

Remember these men:

Kevin Dempsey, Killed In Action, November 13, 2004.
Jonathan Simpson, Killed In Action, October 14, 2006.
Kyle Powell, Killed In Action, November 4, 2006.
Jose Galvan, Killed In Action, November 4, 2006.
Nathan Krisoff, Killed In Action, December 9, 2006.
Gary Johnston, Killed In Action, January 23, 2007.
Dustin Lee, Killed In Action, March 21, 2007.
Luke Milam, Killed In Action, September 25, 2007.
Michael Ferschke, Killed In Action, August 10, 2008.
David Day, Killed In Action, April 24, 2011.

The burden is heavy.

How to Build a Mountain

I built you a mountain today
from the head of a lion,
a pocketful of earth,
and a fist full of my blood.
When I was finished,
the mountain looked at me and said,

I built you a mountain today

I. How to Build a War Machine

Ode to a Pineapple Grenade

Your fingers as lightning bolts
spindle across the sky,
cull skin into a pile,
a rake combing dirt,
softly singing,
All along the watchtower
princes kept their view.
Resurrect your Apocalypse,
sleeping in her white shroud
and nestled in mineral
earth, because war is a performance,
and then we bow.
Black. Curtains. Fire.

Baring the Trees

The dead hang
from the dead like leaves
upon an ashen tree—
waiting for their deep autumn
so that they may open
their withering mouths
and fall, but the sad
season never arrives.

There is always a heavy
heat; always bullets
in a rifle; always a young
finger to slap
the trigger; forever
a fresh body to fasten
a generation.

How to Build a Sand Castle

There was a small island in the middle of a blue ocean.
This island had a beach made of white powdered

sand, but it was not sand—it was something else.
On this island there was a boy. This boy

held a shovel and a pail in his small boy hands.
He spent a warm afternoon building castles

from the sand on his beach, but it was not sand—
it was still something else.

Each time he finished a castle, a wave
would sweep over and knock it down.

Each time a wave knocked down his castle
he would build a taller one.

He built castles until the island was gone, became
the castle. There was only his castle and only the sea.

A little girl emerged from the rough sea, made
of the rough sea.

This is worth dying for
she said, and she opened her mouth

and swallowed the boy whole
because she loved him.

War Haiku

Bullet makers hang
their heads low when they take home
a peasant's wages

Hero's Prayer

I beg that my aim be true and my judgment
sound. When it is my time, let me seep
into the sand amidst a pile of enemies.
Let my barrels be molten and my bayonet
sleep inside insurgent flesh as the backs
of my thumbs run black with powder.
Let glass and shrapnel embed into my skin.
Let my last breath be whispers of curses
and sworn vengeance.

As the rigor washes
over me, turn my smile
to marble, for I have fought
well. Do not let me die
from an incoming mortar round
as I jerk off in the porta-shitter.

Marlboro Man

Where there's smoke—bullshit—*there's fire.*

Where there's smoke,
there's bodies. The fire long gone. Only unfinished
stories remain. Their text poured out upon the—
fuck.

The planted rifle is not a flag. The dog tags can
only hang.
The deeper I breathe, the quicker my cigarette
turns to ash.

Ode to the Enemy Sniper

Searching for your defining
moment, you've come to dance
in our little war. Life is nothing
more than a turn

of the windage knob, a slight
adjustment for distance, a tight
lungful of breath, a sight
bearing black reticle,

that crosshair etched into your lens
like a crucifix, reaching for the edges
of your omniscient circle, a transfer
of kinetic energy from man

to machine to man. The word
Dragunov strikes fear into your enemies,
but in you it triggers
a yearning for combustion, a need for heavy

recoil running deep throughout the recesses
of the body; and so you aim steady, you squeeze
slowly, propelling your projectile towards
the anatomical plexus that turns off the world.

Hookah and Chai

We collided as asteroids
and our skin fell off our bones
in ribbons. The night became
a blanket of dark, sewn with glowing
sand. You groaned

as I reached into your chest
and pumped your heart for you,
because I could. You still taste of stars
and light. In the beginning,

I put the universe into my mouth
and exploded, because I could.
For a second, I was brilliant.

The Imam

I crushed all of your metacarpals
with my outstretched hand
as I stumbled
I brought you down to my eye level.
The corners of your mouth
turned up as grin as your bony splinters
wept marrow and milk.
You laughed:
I can still kneel.

The Platoon Sergeant

You had a pigeon or a child
locked in a wire cage. You fed it glass,
made it do push ups, and kissed it
when you put it to bed.
You taught it to speak.
When it tried to say the word *father*,
you opened the cage—
taught it to fly.

Insurgent

I killed you this morning.
Wait.

I was brought before you. Called upon to nurse your filthy wounds.
I was asked to ease your discomfort in the remaining time

you had on earth. The tender welts across your back revealed how
Iraqi Police questioned you, and why you confessed

to your crime so quickly. You were just a boy. Lucky to own
sixteen years under your olive skin. I bet you felt invincible. Maybe

even brave. The dull opaque color of your hip bone, visible
through the infected hole left by the bullet, whispered

you only had days to live. I begged God to be there when it
happened. I didn't hate you for what you did. I didn't feel much

of anything except burning curiosity. I wanted to unzip you and
place pointy labeled flags into your organs. I needed to see

if your eyes turned to bliss
or fire.

Cylindrical

Between firefights,
those long moments
of silence, of slow
exhale, I allow myself
to grasp a bullet with thumb
and forefinger—
to enjoy its shape, the feel
of its smooth brass
skin against mine.

Holding Maps

I remember the day we learned that our platoon commander had
    no idea
how to read

a map. We followed the streets around in a circle, twice, on a road
    notorious
for buried IEDs.

I developed my first mantra that day. I couldn't stop whispering it.
    It was as simple
as our snatch and grab

mission should have been. As simple as looking at a map. My
    mouth formed shapes
that repeated: *Not my legs.*

Bayonet

We held hands in the dark
while blindfolded
and falling. Our navels
touched and merged
as the world ended
and we began.
In the distance,
we heard music
or screaming.

Lazy Days (Because Killing Is the Easy Part)

On these days we truly suffer;
when our spear-tipped skill sets are not
needed and memories begin to etch
themselves into our skulls
while time slowly crawls

across our skin: some wander
off and call home, some drink
Listerine-flavored vodka. I sit outside
and lazily strum my guitar in time
with the incoming mortar alarms.

Phalanx

They say he ran.

*

He had a first name once, now buried with his honor.
He is merely a rank and a last name. Staff Sergeant _____.

*

They say he ran
      when he saw
            the blast.

*

An action, an impulse. Seduced by lady fear, wearing her gown
of tangibility, speaking materialisms into his ear as she traced

a finger down the slope of his neck and drew a line of succulent
life down to his navel. He looked upon her, lying on the foreign

earth, then draped himself over her. She whispered into his skin
as he covered his *Death Before Dishonor* tattoo in arab mud.

He stretched the night over his face and wept as a child who realizes
that acts have consequences and punishments are real. Death is not

a dream here. There are no monologues, only a violent instant where
our limbs are torn from trunks and we fade as our bodies struggle to

breathe. Our bodies struggle to blink. For those of us who remain
unlucky, we must react. We must close the phalanx. There is still

work to be done. There is still death to gift.

They say he ran
      when he saw
            the blast
                  that killed Gary.

*

And to all those who see Staff Sergeant _____ sitting
behind his little wooden desk, pretending to be a Marine, I beg

you to ask him, "Do you remember Gary Johnston?" And when he
    smirks
and replies, "Yes, I was there the night he died." I want you to look

him in his beady coward eyes and say, "Alpha Company, Third
    Platoon
says go fuck yourself. It should've been you."

Rocket Man

For Corporal Benavidez, affectionately called "Rocket Man" by the platoon after the explosion on December 9, 2006, launched him from his gun turret on the vehicle, through the air, and safely onto the sand fifty meters away.

I dreamed that I opened my mouth and slowly
swallowed an entire rocket.
When I awoke,
I was a rocket.

I had rocket guts and rocket blood.

My rocket feet were plastic fins.
My rocket arms surmounted into steeple.
My rocket hands held a blast wave
and smoke.

I screamed into the earth,
became wind.

War Child

For John "Shooting the Lights Out" Murray, Wounded In Action, October 14, 2010, Afghanistan.

Could you hear the slow hiss
of my hands as they turned
to shrapnel and smoke,
or the sound my heart made
when it collapsed
in on itself?

I'm sorry I wasn't there to save you,
or shoot someone in the face,
or make fun of you for losing
a fight to a bullet,
but most of all,
for not being the one to save you.

Praying Hands as Preparatory Sketch

As if songs were handcuffs
and breaths were beads
sewn unto a dark fabric,
so dark—such fabric.

It is the light friend, light,
friend, that casts itself upon
frozen fields that seeds
may spit and sprout.

Light is a weapon. Tongues
are a weapon. And hands
were made to ball
and strike and pray.

Soft Walls

For Binyam Jimma, Wounded In Action, November 23, 2006.

I ain't never been to Baghdad.
By the time I arrived, the walls
were too soft. I'm a boy

of the small town, where
the dirty fight lurks,
and the earth beneath

the road swells pregnant
with anger. I'm a boy
of the outskirts,

where a faint and distant pop
can steal your arms and legs
like it did to Jimma as the bullet

bit and kicked
his spinal cord to ribbons,
and the tenth man in a patrol

will suddenly blink at you
from the half of his face
that is now lying

on the ground. I'm a boy
of the sand dune,
where fire claims skin

and RPGs dance over plumes.
No, I ain't never been to Baghdad.
The walls were too soft.

How to Man a Rampart

The stars are made of fire tonight, you said, as you put on your coat,
sewn from the foam of a rough sea.

We were standing on a castle wall, above an armada of advancing
enemy ships, because there are always

advancing enemy ships. *They seem cleaner this time,* I said, my arms
outstretched, trying to embrace anything, looking

out upon our empire of ocean. You reached out for my hand,
interlocking our fingers, like a marriage,

but forever. You wanted to say *I love you* but your mouth was full of
glowing embers, spilling hot ash upon the ground.

I Wasn't Always a Desert

I dreamed that I opened my mouth and slowly
swallowed an entire country.
When I awoke,
I was Iraq.

So I began to oppress myself.
I took away my electricity, my gasoline,
and I cut off the heads of my children.

I became
arid.

II. I Painted Myself (Burning)

The Marriage of Hand and Spear

*T.J. "Laser" Edwards, our radio chief, was severely burned over 45 percent
of his body by an Improvised Explosive Device on Dec. 9, 2006. When I
had finished the deployment, I called him up as he was recovering at
the Brooke Army Medical Center. We had a conversation full of sarcasm,
just like old times. But then he became silent, and ended our conversation
with, "Doc, I still have these dreams. Every night I watch myself
burning. Every night I re-live the burn, and every night it
is you that throws the match and laughs."*

Our legs as matchsticks, sifting the orange filth and
debris of last conversations written upon trodden

and upturned faces. We chop the stalks of paper
flowers and sit on mounds of Molotov dirt as we

futilely wind clockworks.
We fear the holes that leak and swallow and weep.

We fear the cured skins hanging from dried thatch.
And we stride upon eyes, converse with our smiles

atop a film of blue water. We sleep, as we have been
conditioned, to the gentle suction sound of our tongues

being pulled apart by caked hands and then washed in a
riot of flame.

As the rivers turn to marsh and reed, my hands laugh
and smile as they peel back the folds of flesh in play,

as hands are known to do. "If there was no war, there
would be no bravery."

Sundays

She folds the laundry neatly, letting
the warmth from the dryer envelop
her soft hands. He kicks
back the recliner, a fresh
beer opened, getting ready
to watch some football. Two men
in military uniforms

ring the doorbell.

Memorial Day

I sit with my barrel chest,
my steel pipe arms,
my head burrowed
into calloused hands.

The ice cubes clink
in an empty glass
and beg the bottle of Glenfiddich
for a refill, to forgive
the abandonment and remember
the fading faces
of my friends that are
now just granite
and pitied whispers
on a single day of the year.

How to Paint Fallujah as Still Life

There was an island in the middle of a blue ocean. It was covered
in that white powdered sand that was not

sand, it was something else. There was also that tree, the one that
bore fruit, but it was not actually fruit, it was tiny

elephant bones. And there was that girl, the one from the sea who
is made of the sea, spinning tight concentric

circles, coaxing her dress, the one that sang out in emerald, to
flourish around her, embroidering the air

with a soft salt spray. And of course there was the boy, that
determined sand castle builder, sitting cross-legged,

smiling dumbly at her, chewing on a piece of light, not questioning
why there were stars in his mouth.

Kevin Dempsey

My dive partner throughout the Marine Corps Combatant Diver Course,
Killed In Action, November 13, 2004, Al Anbar Province, Iraq.

I saw you today, wearing
a SCUBA tank and holding
a harpoon or a map.
You opened your mouth
as if to say something but it was lost
in the hum of the gathering crowd.
We watched as you leapt
off the earth's edge—there was no splash.

Jose Galvan

Killed In Action, November 4, 2006.

The frozen grass gives way under
heavy soles. Tears turn to ice before
they shatter upon the ground.
Corporal Jose Galvan does not blink.
The flag keeps his coffin warm.

The Sound of

Raindrops on roses and whiskers on kittens, these are a few of my favorite things (Sound of Music).

I saw a kitten
once, sauntering down the dusty streets

of Fallujah.
Its gray fur was matted to its body and it stunk

of sulfur.
Its eyes spoke of fear or love or vengeance.

Its pads
were torn and splayed and it gingerly pranced

down the alleyway—
danced over the garbage. When it saw us,

it let out
a moan, or a howl, or a laugh.

Nathan Krisoff

Killed In Action, December 9, 2006.

The Van Gogh *Starry Night* begins to drip with dark hued blues while hazy golden rays peek over a sleepy and hollow horizon. Tendrils of a decaying lavender slither away from the rising sun with siren songs of lament in their hearts and sharpened shivs behind their backs.

The sun cautiously crawls through two twin billows of white smoke emanating from the worn brick towers of a nearby power plant. The aroma of freshly brewed coffee rides the wisps of wind around my porch and settles in a chipped mug that's branded *Reconnaissance Marine*.

The grass begins to sparkle with its bounty of dew that was stolen from the sweet and unsuspecting air the darkness prior. I sit on a throne of wood and apathy as the lingering remnants of a long and arduous night of drinking cheap vodka courses up and around the pommel of my throbbing temples.

The cherry of my Marlboro glows a bright orange and defies the sneaking dawn's cool morning vapors as I witness the skyward changing of the guard.

I know this sunrise. I know this sky. It's the exact same painting I witnessed two years ago in the sands of Iraq. I remember that morning vividly, as a fireball bloomed from the under-carriage of the second vehicle in our convoy as they ran over a cunningly hidden IED.

Those same rays of golden light breaking over a thick onyx tower of smoke from the vehicle that melted down to flecks of steel. I tried to run into the swell of blue fire to pull out Nate's trapped body but was tackled and restrained by Sgt. Maxwell as I beat my fists upon his face and chest.

44

I helplessly watched Nate's skin ooze down to the crystalline sand floor through the tears in my eyes that belonged on a face much older, much wiser. And when it was over, and the vehicle was reduced to glowing embers, I sat on a throne of sand and sorrow with my vacant stare of defeat.

And the cherry of my Marlboro glowed a bright orange and defied the sneaking dawn's cool morning vapors as I witnessed the skyward changing of the guard.

Dreams of Brass

I dreamed that I opened my mouth and slowly
swallowed brass.
When I awoke,
I was a bullet.

My bullet arms raised high in a V,
my bullet feet stamped with a 5.56,
I spiraled blindly through the air.

I swam into the skin of your chest.
I swam into your muscle and marrow.
I swam into the chambers of your heart.
You were full of knives—questions.

Posthumous

I built you this
evening from a used hypodermic
needle and pieces of dove.
We sat and stared at each

other. You commented
that I was already
dead. I commented
I'd already loved you.

Dustin Lee

Killed In Action, March 21, 2007.

Babies swaddled in electrical wires suckle from the caps of primed detonators as we march through Elysian fields of broken radio parts and ancient blast holes.

We gallop between the crests of rolling sand dunes in Clydesdale up-armored trucks with wild manes of chain-linked bullets blowing in the stifling hot breeze.

Steel triggers wrap around calloused fingers as boys turn to hardened men in the squeeze of an instant. And there, in the distance, the enemy rocket slowly

spirals as it steers itself towards its target. Dustin Lee slumps against the concrete wall like a weather-beaten traveler upon a bar stool as the shrapnel

from the blast sneaks by his body armor, puncturing both lungs and shredding arteries and organs beyond repair on its bouncing trajectory throughout

his chest cavity. His grip upon my arm slowly wanes and his pupils begin to grow until they're the size of black silver dollars. We all know how this will end.

Six months into this deployment and we've been here before, several times. It ends with the lowest ranking Marine uncoiling the hose and pressure-washing

the remaining blood and froth that has intimately bonded to the seams of earth and stone. It ends by expending an entire can of Febreeze to hide the smell of death and failure. It ends with a *Fuck*, a *Goddamnit!*, a *Why him?*, a few tears, and then a cigarette. It ends with another reason to pull the trigger.

He was twenty years old.

War Haiku (B-Side)

Out of work artists
sculpt beauty into bullets
and paint the war blue.

Gary Johnston

Killed In Action, January 23, 2007.

The creak and groan
of this barstool lets me know
that it had a life
before me. Just boys

then, as our deeds flew
higher than our dreams
meant them to.
I still taste the metallic ash

as we plummeted back to the earth
and black flowers encased
our bodies, cushioned our fall
against God's hand.

Now I stand alone at January's end—
I witness your face
in the reflection of clear
cylindrical glass.

Do you remember the last thing you said to me?

You called me an *asshole*
in your small-town southern accent
and we laughed until you drifted
beyond my reach.

We were beautiful then.

How to Paint a Burning

I painted a city.
In this city, I painted a minaret.
On this minaret, I painted a fresco
of you on the wall.
You were descending a spiral staircase
but it wasn't enough.
I painted myself burning
down the minaret.

So I painted a city.
In this city, I painted a minaret burning.
Outside of the minaret, I painted myself,
painting myself,
painting you.
You are always descending.
There is always a fire.

How to Lace Light

FADE IN: AERIAL EXTREME LONG SHOT: Night. Camera sweeps over a small island in a dark ocean. The island is covered by an ancient castle that is overrun with ivy on every surface. All lighting is from the torches that line the castle walls and courtyard and a full moon in the sky. There are dead bodies and weapons covering the ramparts and courtyard grounds.

CUT TO: LONG SHOT of COURTYARD. There is a young man writhing in the courtyard next to a large tree. He is holding a small red plastic pail in his left hand, a blood-covered sword in his right hand, and he looks like you. There is a young woman with chestnut brown hair that falls in waves to her shoulders and is wearing a coat made from the foam of a rough sea. She is kneeling next to the man, his head cradled in her lap. She is caressing his hair, and she also looks like you.

VOICE-OVER (WOMAN)

I watched you dying slowly, holding your abdomen as if it were perfect, or punctured. You looked at me and said: *We are all made of star stuff, the light and the pulling,* and then you were silent, because long dramatic monologues are cliché, and you were above speaking over the wind.

CUT TO: CLOSE UP of MAN'S leather boots. The camera pans slowly from his feet to his head as woman continues voice-over. His body is still slowly writhing.

VOICE-OVER (WOMAN)

My eyes swept over your body. It was slowly pulsing, slowly expanding, slowly being consumed by a bright light from your insides that you could no longer contain. I watched your skin flake off into swirling golden dust as rays sprang into the night.

CUT TO: CLOSE UP of WOMAN'S hands caressing MAN'S hair. Camera pans slowly up to her face while she continues voice-over. Her lips do not move.

VOICE-OVER (WOMAN)

I wanted to be pure like you, like light—like you—and do star things, like you, so I laced the roof of my mouth with the strands of light pouring forth from your guts.

We were joined, like fabric, or hands, but it was not enough to keep you.

Woman looks upwards towards the sky.

Camera pans quickly upwards to a starry night sky. In the background there is the sound of children laughing.

FADE OUT.

So I Was a Coffin

For Kyle Powell, died in my arms, November 4, 2006.

They said *you are a spear.* So I was a spear.

I walked around Iraq upright and tall, but the wind began to blow
    and I began
to lean. I leaned into a man, who leaned into a child, who leaned
into a city. I walked back to them and neatly presented a city of
    bodies
packaged in rows. They said *no. You are a bad spear.*

They said *you are a flag.* So I was a flag.

I climbed to the highest building, in the city that had no bodies,
    and I smiled
and waved as hard as I could. I waved too hard and I caught fire
    and I burned
down the city, but it had no bodies. They said *no. You are a bad flag.*

They said *you are a bandage.* So I was a bandage.

I jumped on Kyle's chest and wrapped my lace arms together
around his torso and pressed my head to his ribcage and listened to
his heartbeat. Then I was full, so I let go and wrung myself out.

And I jumped on Kyle's chest and wrapped my lace arms together
around his torso and pressed my head to his ribcage and listened to
his heartbeat. Then I was full, so I let go and wrung myself out.

And I jumped on Kyle's chest and wrapped my lace arms together
around his torso and pressed my head to his ribcage but there was
no heartbeat. They said *no. You are a bad bandage.*

They said *you are a coffin.* So I was.

I found a man. They said he died bravely, or he will. I encom-
  passed him
in my finished wood, and I shut my lid around us. As they lowered us
into the ground he made no sound because he had no eyes
and could not cry. And as I threw dirt upon us we held our breaths
  together
and they said, *yes. You are a good coffin.*

Eulogy (Originally read at the Memorial For Corporal Dustin Lee)

Before I ever knew what poetry was, or took a class or workshop through a university, these were my words. This will forever be my most honest and raw piece of work. These words were borne from the thoughts and minds of the men of Third Reconnaissance Battalion. These words blanket our dead. Rest in peace, brothers.

How can you know what sharing is, if you've never given your last dessert to a friend?

How can you know what laughter is, if you've never been so miserable, the only thing left to do is laugh?

How can you know what failure is, if despite all your training, you still have to hold a brother during his last breaths?

How can you know what hate is, if you've never cursed God and His will?

How can you know what a brother is, if you've never had one taken from you?

This is war. It doesn't matter if it's right. It doesn't matter if we believe in it. It only matters that we're here.

Home is a distant memory.

Family is the man ducking down next to you.

You're only as good as your last mission and your sole existence is to complete the next one.

Those of us that live through this will die in our beds, forgotten.

Those of us that gave all will be remembered forever.

III. *Welcome Home, or the Sound of Your Blood Humming*

Zipper

The war has
seared through
me like a jagged
unsightly scar,
running down
the middle
of my body,
holding it,
together.

The Dangers of Time Travel

You wake up in the future and realize that everyone has evolved. People now have the head of a blue jay and the body of a shiny machine that whirs softly as its insides spin. You see two bird heads that look like your parents, but, of course, that is not possible.

When they see you, they cry and shake their heads slowly with disappointment because you are not like them. *I'm sorry,* you say, your voice rough and hard from one thousand years of sleeping. *We are all dying,* they sing, their voices like glockenspiels.

War Junkie

I drank from your hand, cupped—
the shape of a well—water spilling over
the lip, prostrate upon the earth.

I called out your name, shouting thickly—
the cool air pressing heavy—a night
ready for noise.

I bound myself to you, knotted—
two bodies intertwined in a plot—a fraying
rope, a mouthless:

I loved you.

The Thousand-Yard Stare

I built a wall from pieces
of an old wall and mortar made
from your ground up skin.

Then I carved the shape
of your face into my arm
but my arm became glass

and your face became sand.
I placed this wall on the moon
or some other far away place

so that when it falls
there is nothing I can do
to stop it.

Commandment

Do you remember the morning
we awoke and you asked:
thou shalt not kill?
I stretched and flexed my arms as hard as I could.
I cut my palm to the bone and smeared
thou shalt not kill
on the wall above our bed.

Do you remember the morning
we awoke and you asked:
why should we not kill
as you left?
I whispered
because it is written,
but it wasn't.

Painting the War Blue

Your fingers as knives
swarthing the air,
cutting holes into the fabric

of atmosphere, hanging
constellations from the torn flaps
of universe and dust and matter.

I watched you pluck the tiniest
star from the sky. It was the size—
shape, of a brightly glowing apple

resting in the palm.
I watched you run a finger
clockwise around the skin,

pulling apart the two halves of rind.
I watched you put the globes of light
into your mouth and swallow because

we prayed it so. I watched you jump
into the night and become a nebula because we prayed
it so. When no one is looking, I reach

for you. I stretch my fingers and cry
out, startling owls. My arm grows one centimeter
longer each time. I miss your heat; your breath.

Flashback

What a surprise this morning
when I rolled over to watch you sleep
and I realized your face
had become a mandala.
It was the most beautiful I had ever seen
you. You were a sacred space.
You were a pinnacle.
I left before you awoke
but I imagine that you wept
and clawed upon seeing your face
in the mirror and realizing that
it had become a cosmos.

Prelude in E-Minor (op. 28, no. 4)

I closed my eyes for a second in the lull
of a warm evening. And out beyond
the dusk and haze of the slowly setting
sun, someone began playing Chopin.

So I donned my alpine white
Les Paul guitar and plugged
my quarter-inch cable
into a Marshal half-stack,

cranking the distortion and creating
a crisp static buzz. I palm-muted
and percussed the strings until I answered
with a song of longing—of rifle fire.

The Bullet Maker

My body is strong
from a lifetime of climbing
and picking bushels of cold light,
placing them in a basket,
leaving holes in the sky. I forged
you a bullet from brass
and my precious light.
When you died
I buried you with it.
Here Lies a Bullet and Light
On your gravestone there is frost
and night.

From Agamemnon to Menelaus, or How to Eat Rocks

Do you remember when we were children, before all this war, before all this sacrifice, and we would run down from the Grecian hinterlands and across the powdered white sands and kick our feet into the foam tips of small waves as they crawled up the beach to die before returning to the swirling churn? I asked you if you'd ever eat a rock sandwich, and you laughed and said no, and that it would break all of your teeth, as if a mouth with more room for echo was the worst thing that could happen to us?

I wanted you to say yes.

I wanted you to hold my hand as we closed our eyes and swallowed those rocks because what if they did not break our teeth, but instead slid smooth into the depths of our bellies and there blossomed until they filled our abdomens—became our insides—became our outsides.

And what if we kept growing, kept becoming more stone and more earth, grew to something grand and sculpted like a fjord?

Gut Shot

I shot a man in the stomach
this morning. I watched
his blood fall: dark, soft,
chimney soot powder.

Why did you do that?

asked my tiny wife. Her hands
smoking pistols.

Because he wronged me.

The words left my mouth, but it was not
my voice. It was deeper and heavy, so
very heavy.

How did he wrong you?

asked my hands
as pistols, tiny wife.

He carved a hole in the ocean.

She laughed, a wind chime,
and kissed my cheek.

Mouths

You opened your beautiful,
beautiful mouth and dream spilt
out. Slow—lazy. Dripping, a shimmering
pool that collected itself into
a younger you. A you before
the war—that young face—
whispering: *I am a chrysalis*

but my hands are so small.
And your hands were so small.
And we laughed until you aged,
until you became half moon
and half fire, until you devoured
that insignificant city and then wrapped
me up tightly in your arms, slowly

constricting, trying to splinter
my ribs, waiting for me to exhale, needing
my breath to fill your beautiful,
beautiful mouth, but my beautiful,
beautiful mouth was cinched.
Then my lungs burst, unribboning
themselves into thousands

of tiny plum blossoms, and my bones,
hollow and bird-like, became tiny plum blossoms,
and my skin, thin as papyrus, became
tiny plum blossoms, and my eyes, full
of pith and home, became tiny plum
blossoms, and all I could see for miles
and miles were tiny plum blossoms. The moon

half of you loved this, and the fire
half did not, so you opened your beautiful,
beautiful mouth and sang out

until you became half
crest and half spill
as you swept away a city
of ash and plum blossoms.

War Junkie (Reprise)

I could not remember your face
      but I wanted to, so I built
            a tree of tiny plum blossoms

      that I found floating in puddles
upon the ground. I created
      a breeze so that this tree would dance

and sway. I forged a sun
      so that it would have rays of light
to reach for or bask in. And finally,

           I built a second tree out of the tiny
      elephant bones floating in the air.
The trees were just out of each

other's reach, which made
their love strong. The shape
of our faces no longer mattered.

Tracer

Like a bluejay. Silhouette. Embroidered against a sharp city skyline at night in November. And let's say there's a thick darkness. And let's say that it's winter. Snow. Or still snowing. And now there's this coldness that's implied as you create constellations while screaming towards a hazy horizon.

That's where you are.

You are glittering now, or glass-like, or you are a solid onyx citadel.

You are unsure of yourself. The opacity of your skin changing with every breath of frigidly condensed air on its way out of mouth and into merciless atmosphere.

You want to be a kaleidoscope, bathing people in patterns and colors. You want to be that perfect telescope. The one with a sharp lens that can only look forward, towards the future, towards the twinkling stars that are really just explosions and dying light.

Instead, you are simply a wall of dead bodies. Some still twitching, their nervous systems in spasm, not realizing that they're inanimate, that they're supposed to lie still, supposed to be beautiful.

Of course you did not kill them all. No, that would make you a monster. But you are one of many inciting incidents.

And if you could just hold your head higher when you cry—because the masses love sadness—and if the bodies that now make up your arms, your legs, your writhing ribcage would just stop moving and moaning, you could be loved, studied, worshipped, and be worth more than just the burning of parts.

The Dangers of Time Travel (Reprise)

You wake up in the future and realize that everyone has devolved. People now have gills and fishtails and fins. Everyone is underwater. You are now underwater. This ocean is the color of decaying leaves and right now this is beautiful.

You want to have a child. You want to see your reflection in something that grows and grows. You want to sing. Your mouth full of song as the rusty sea begins to rattle. You want the shaking to stop but it devours you.

The Killhole

He strikes the match and watches the flame dance and flicker,
splashing light upon deeds that stretch all the way to an exhausted

heart. His body grinds out menial tasks among the hanging wires,
hardhats, and drill guns while His mind returns to the killhole.
    Tears are His

bullets. Revenge is His rifle. His bones wait for a revolution,
any excuse to oppress. His faith is an underscore to duty. Beneath
    His skin

He knows that houses are built upon hate and Iraqi children
make excellent mortar. At the end of the day, He still searches for
    dead bodies

behind the drywall. At home, a baby bawls and reaches
for His rough hand. With a gentle rocking and rough lullaby, the
    crying stops.

The pacifier smells like whiskey.

How to Genesis

In the middle of a blue ocean
there was an old castle made
of sand—but it was not sand,

it was something else. It had towers,
ramparts, waves of ivy, and a drawbridge—all
things a respectable castle should have.

In the courtyard
was a large tree bearing
fruit. But it was not fruit—

it was tiny elephant bones.
There was a small girl
from a rough sea, made of a rough sea,

who walked around the tree humming
a war hymn, but not loud enough to discover
which one. She picked a piece of fruit

and brought it to her mouth, parted
her lips and blew out towards the water
with her breezy breath, watching

it break into shards, setting each bone
adrift upon the wind the way
a dandelion explodes itself to live.

And as each tiny bone touched
the water it grew into its own tiny island
with its own tiny tree and its own tiny fruit.

When she had finished, she had created
an archipelago. In this way,
a world was born.

Survivor's Guilt

—Summary of Awards Submission

Rank: PO3
Name: Gerardo Mena
Recommendation: Navy Achievement Medal with Combat
Distinguishing Device
Action Period: 20060930-20070417
Status: Completed
Last Updated By: Awards Admin on 07/23/2007 02:39:36 PM
Last Forwarded To: HQMC Military Awards Branch on
07/11/2007
Final Approved Award: NV
Date Approved: 07/11/2007 03:48:19 PM
Approved By: Brian McLaughlin, Major, On behalf of Major
General Walter E. Gaskin, Commanding General, II MEF FWD
Summary Action: Hospital Corpsman Third Class Mena was in
receipt of Imminent Danger Pay during this period.
Recommended Citation:

HEROIC ACHIEVEMENT IN THE SUPERIOR PERFOR-
MANCE OF HIS DUTIES WHILE SERVING AS CORPS-
MAN, COMPANY A, 3D RECONNAISSANCE BATTALION,
REGIMENTAL COMBAT TEAM 6, II MARINE EXPEDI-
TIONARY FORCE (FORWARD) FROM SEPTEMBER 2006
TO APRIL 2007 IN SUPPORT OF OPERATION IRAQI
FREEDOM 05-07 AND 06-08. HOSPITAL CORPSMAN
THIRD CLASS MENA'S PLATOON BENEFITED FROM HIS
EXEMPLARY MEDICAL PERFORMANCE THROUGH-
OUT THE DEPLOYMENT DURING NUMEROUS MIS-
SIONS AND COMBAT OPERATIONS. ON 4 NOVEMBER,
2006, HE RESPONDED TO AN IMPROVISED EXPLOSIVE
DEVICE ATTACK THAT KILLED ONE MARINE AND
SEVERELY WOUNDED ANOTHER. WITHOUT HESITA-
TION, HE MOVED INTO THE KILL ZONE AND WORKED
FERVENTLY TO SAVE THE WOUNDED MARINE'S

LIFE. HIS COURAGEOUS ACTION FACILITATED THE EVACUATION OF THE INJURED MARINE TO A SURGICAL CENTER WITHIN MINUTES OF THE ATTACK. ON 9 DECEMBER 2006, THE COMMAND AND CONTROL VEHICLE IN HIS PLATOON STRUCK AN IMPROVISED EXPLOSIVE DEVICE. HE QUICKLY SEIZED CONTROL OF THE SCENE AND COORDINATED THE TREATMENT AND RAPID EVACUATION OF FIVE WOUNDED MARINES. HOSPITAL CORPSMAN THIRD CLASS MENA'S INITIATIVE, PERSEVERANCE, AND TOTAL DEDICATION TO DUTY REFLECTED CREDIT UPON HIM AND WERE IN KEEPING WITH THE HIGHEST TRADITIONS OF THE UNITED STATES NAVAL SERVICE.

The Spent

It seems so long ago since we spilt
our bloom, sculpted our sleep
around the impact of ricochets
into powdered dust, cried out *Mene Mene*
as we waded into the Tigris

to recover bodies. This is not
the first time I have spoken
of this. And each time the story grows
less. Grows thin. Each time I end
with a sigh, the only honest breath

from my lungs, borne of a lexicon of light
breathing, these tiny learned exhalations
covering the holes that now stipple
my stories—that have displaced
those moments when I cried out:

forgive me